SELF-ROMANCING

by L SCULLY

DOPAMINE
BOOKS AND PRINTED MATTER

Published by DOPAMINE
301 N. Kenwood St, Glendale, CA 91206
www.dopaminepress.org

Covert Art: Cate White
Layout & Design: Brooke Palmieri

ISBN: 978-1-63590-263-1
Distributed by the MIT Press, Cambridge, Mass., and London, England.
Printed in the United States of America

10 9 8 7 6 5 4 3 2 1

Praise for *Self-Romancing*

"To those who have never believed poetry can be a page-turner, may you get to turning! The addictive reading of this brilliant poetry collection is a testament to the ears and breath aligned with the music L Scully joins for us at every corner of our imaginations. This book is like dreaming alongside a giant who is a farmer who used to be a flower who used to be a stack of typed pages. Dream and turn onward! I'm a fan of this colossal opening the poems make around the heart so it may grow, and much gratitude Dear Poet!"
—CAConrad, author of *Listen to the Golden Boomerang Return*

"I'm enchanted by the voice of L Scully's 'self-romancing,' the frisky and tender way they speak to themselves and their lovers, friends, dog. Each page reads like its own playhouse built by queer joy, grief, meditations on excess, and the risks and worth-its of intimacy. I needed these spells, will keep them close."
—K Iver, author of *Short Film Starring My Beloved's Red Bronco*

"Mere chants for abundance, purpose, and destiny are ASMR-ed mouth sounds compared to the churning life force of L Scully's poetically packed take on affirmations. A parataxic pileup of wry, twisted, and poignant lines that turn maxims, aphorisms, and apothegms into inverted declarations of a voracious shape-shifting self. Part Nathalie Sarraute's *Tropisms*, part Joe Brainard's *I Remember*, this book pulses with electric sensation and stray-thought beauty."
—Nate Lippens, author of *Ripcord*

"In *Self-Romancing*, L Scully spills their guts with brutal clarity, humor, and astonishing precision. Unsparing and sly, this is a book that refuses to look away—and you won't be able to, either."
—Elaine Kahn, author of *Romance or The End*

A stranger has come
To share my room in the house not right in the head . . .
—Dylan Thomas, "Love in the Asylum"

DOGS are NOT allowed on the tennis courts!
—the tennis courts

I am in control of my own fate. I am in love with my friends and un-in love with everyone who is bad for me. It doesn't matter that I missed the green comet this morning. Harm reduction is prevalent in my self-actions. I am a good person. I am a good lay. It's not important whether I'm a good lay. It's hot when I mention the psych ward on Hinge. The copper in my body is actively preventing pregnancy. I am not trans only because I dressed up as Peter Pan for six halloweens in a row. My Capricornian ambition extends beyond the frameworks of late-stage capitalism. I am capable of having a job to support my dog son. I am allowed to kiss for free.

I am not saving myself for marriage but I am saving myself for correctness. It's okay that my hair isn't as orange as it used to be. Hazelnut is not an allergy of mine. I keep learning. I am capable of not having sex on the first date. I do not look like every other ginger twink. I do not have to like eels. If I were a fruit I'd be a strawberry even though that isn't necessarily my favorite or even the most accurate fruit. I do not have to indulge in fiction of any kind. I am on a path to achieve my dreams. I am learning how to, in the words of Maya Skylark, "romanticize solitude."

I have many good qualities other than dancing. My bottom lip is provocative in the right quantity. I do not sound like a fin-de-siècle psychoanalysis patient when I complain. He/theys love me. I am allowed to be resentful about my period. I am also allowed to drink sweet and delicious things as breakfast. I am worth a double text. I am an adult and can eat candy that compromises my enamel if I so choose. My enamel is not thinning. Cats are neutral creatures that do not have a vendetta against me. My ass pays my utilities. The little berries on the side of the road are not all over my shoes and dog. It is not a sinister omen that my left eye can't stop crying. I am good at being gay.

I can stop myself from hurting someone before they can hurt me. It is not abnormal that I jerk off until I cry. Crying is a good thing because it means your emotions are working, even when you do it ugly. Menswear should not be the default for clothed androgyny. I am allowed to want both top surgery and a boob job. That being said, my tits are perfect. I'm allowed to get mad when people I don't know talk to me about my tits. It's okay that I can't love you romantically. I would rather die in a submarine than outer space.

I will probably not die from lack of sleep. My new orange slippers will not clash with my sexy pajama collection. I am allowed to send one regrettable text per day. I am not allergic to cum. Actually I am allergic to cum but the hives aren't that bad. I can have cum hives on my chest if I so choose as long as they are not preemptive to anaphylaxis. Someone is going to gift me roses one day soon. Blood is in some ways equal to the thickness of water. I know what "meniscus" means. I am worth a second date. My worth is not defined by dates. I seem shorter in person.

I am what you see. Coregulation is within reach. My earliest childhood memory is not about peeing in a cup. Eating soap is not a sin. Hardly anything is a sin and I would know as a devout sinner. I can take a day off of sex. I am expanding and evaporating constantly and at the same time. Whipped cream is not unsafe for dogs. I can keep my shorts on when I want to. I field many international calls. Earth signs aren't blameless regardless of what the snail in my ear tells me. I am not Bad. I am just a person. I am probably in love with you. In fact I am.

I will receive a big kiss very soon. There are worse things than muddy paws. There are also worse things than cum in your hair. Pomegranate seeds will not curse me. No one will sue me for defamation in my lifetime. My dermatillomania is not gross and distracting. It's okay that I only got to Step Three. Influencers can't hurt me. Some candles have no smell. I go by Babygirl and still I rescind my womanhood. It's alright to miss it sometimes. I have received so many kisses this year I can't even count. I am a good slut but not the way men whisper in my bedroom. I do not see my ex-girlfriend in my dreams! One cheese stick at a time.

I will prove I know how to love tonight. My heart is not irreparably broken. Having sex in the living room is A-okay. I do not play the same record for every boy that comes over. I can have mixed feelings on rose gold as a concept. I am my own type of polyamorous. One day I will have a big fish tank. My tits are equally hot in lingerie or a binder. I am not going to Hell. Hell is not real but in the caverns of my mind. I can give in if I don't make a big deal about it. I am capable of going to the dentist platonically. My passions will be returned. I will not run out of quarters.

I am wholly loved and wholly sad. One day someone will ask to hold my hand. One day someone will love me so much. One day someone will love me. And it will be So. Much.

I am not the only gay person at the function. Fortified orange juice is not a meal. I did not throw out your toothbrush. The glass of water next to my bed is not dusty. Your glass of water next to my bed isn't either. Bull mastiffs love me. I made a new friend. My new friend might be reading this now. If you're a new friend I love you and you are welcome here. I am a good friend indeed.

I can have the same flavor palate as my dog. People make mistakes. I do not owe everyone $200. I am allowed to weep publicly should I need to. I am the most popular dog dad at the tennis courts. My love language is walking you to the skate park. Hummus will heal me today. You're going to message me back. I am owed nothing and yet I am getting Something. I am a connector of people and things. I am a conduit for better items of the universe. I love the whoosh of trains. You are not channeling negative perceptions toward me as you read this. Your silence is benevolent. I can wait until you come out. I can wait.

I know how many stops are on the orange line. I do not bathe too much. I want to bathe in your shadow.

I am blinking like an automated speed meter. I did not make a rookie mistake with my love this morning. I am a summation of my cohort of mother figures even when I don't like it. I did not cry angry tears to sleep last night. I am wearing sparkly socks for the sheer festivity of it. I am not in the hospital. I will stay out of the hospital this upcoming Pisces season. When I turn on the shower I smell my grandmother's laundry detergent if I turn my nose just so. I am not devastated by loss. My grief grows flowers like the graveyards of Berlin. I only like songs that are about love. I only like poems that are about love. I only like you when you're about love.

Evenings can't be lonely because they are just evenings. The mini roses from Trader Joe's are a little bit much for me. Not everyone has a middle name. I have a middle name and it is Rose, I'm not sure if I told you but now you know. I am not lost within my own roster of pseudonyms. I am what my grandmother wished for. You are going to acknowledge my vulnerable email. You are going to watch this Instagram story and miss me. A queer future is the only future I want. I am not madly in love with someone disinterested. I am humbled by my addictions. Professionalism can't hurt me. The aching never stops but here I am! I am not going to like my therapist on Hinge. I am a good girl without the girl part. Pink is not a bad color for me. I will not check if you've seen my message. I will not beg for love. I am not above anything but my face could be above yours. I don't always need a hand to hold. At the same time if you wanted to hold my hand, just ask.

I almost did not know love or literature if it wasn't for you. I almost did not know! I want to lick the bones of your hips as they cup my face. I want to cum at the same time across time and its space. I think of you when I turn on the shower. I think of you when I turn off the shower. I think of you when I slide my palms up my thighs in bed at night. I do not think of you while I'm being taken but yes yes I do. I think of you as the profiterole of gender. As my future boywife. As the Salem tide as it ebbs and flows against my cold-toed deathwish. I write you something every day. Even when I do not write to you I am writing to you. It is every day now. I would learn to cook you something, though all I can offer is bread. Let me take your body like the bread I received on my lips for so many young years. I like it when you take off your shirt. I aspire for you to take off mine in tandem. You almost make me want to ride a bicycle. I'd hold your hand across our bicycles if I remembered how to ride. I know how to ride you perfectly. I learned long ago in an arboretum before I met you. When I used to fuck my pillows the ghost of you was in my head. I drew you on the floor.

Your name ejaculates the rush of love into my sorry heart. You make my heart un-sorry. Let me introduce you to my family, through a letter or a mirror or the flesh. I thought of you the night of my graduation. I always think of you at night. I fear I always will! The anarchy of your devotion and the emailed love letters make me want to rethink underwear. I will work hard so I can take you to dinner in London. I will work hard for you in the way that isn't work at all. This is a love note that you asked for but I would have written anyway. I am reading your hands in gratitude. Our hands will touch our shaky hands.

I am entitled to artificial flavoring. Intimacy is making its way to me. I am not being ghosted. Actually yes I am and that's okay. I am being ghosted and that's okay. My dog did not eat a used condom and then shit it out completely. Not everyone on earth has my nudes. I am crafting a community guidelines post that men will adhere to. I am not blocked by people I love. The love I fell in yesterday will carry me through a lonely evening.

I am going to engage in heavy kissing this evening. I am not toxic for listening to the entire discography of Green Day. People would have held my hand at Friday night skate in middle school had I asked. I have not been fixated on the skin beneath breasts since childhood. I know how to drive even though I choose not to. I can drive if you've been drinking. Two hospitals ago got bad google ratings but I made the best of it. I like girls with green hair. You will delight in me at tonight's open mic. I will be showered with opportunity that translates to a CV. I am not branded by your escape. I am branded by my own. I am not nauseated by rejection of any sort. I am capable of talking to children one on one. If my hair was long enough you'd braid it. Never mind that it will never be long again. My mother did not cry when I cut it off. You are ignoring me for good reason. I ignored you first. I will never live with a romantic partner. Okay maybe I will if someone wanted to live with me. We will have separate bedrooms. I will not fuck your roommate. I will not! I am blessed by the luck of ladybugs. Did you know I call them ladybirds? I do not call them that for attention. I just say some things funny because of the British thing. The tattoo on my chest is for my grandmother. The tattoo on my chest is not a target for when you finish on me. The tattoo on my chest is close to my heart.

I am lucky beyond measure! I am not just saying that because of the orgasm I had last night. (But it did help.) I am the embodiment of your desire. I am even the embodiment of mine. I have daylight coming to me. I wear platforms so I can kiss you better. I am struck with the mourning of your body and feel it in my own. Whole Foods pizza tastes like Naples. You could never keep up with me! My want was not too big. I am not fucking a thousand people to see if one of them fucks like you. I am not in mourning. Anniversaries are just days. I am no longer interested in Aquarians. People will attend my workshop! You have not forgotten me. We will create beautiful things together aside from babies. I am the very babe of my own workshop. I did not attend the meeting with hickeys. I don't wear hickeys like a giddy teenager. I don't want your marks all over me like a brand. (Yes I do.) My inbox will be respectful today. I will be paid for my troubles. I am more of a boy than you think. Your ex could never! I don't open my window for you in every dream. I don't need to be a sexy cyclist. Some music just hurts. My gender is not isolating. I have a thousand loves. I fuck you like you're one of them. Maybe you are! There's no "we" in "tiramisu" but there is almost an "Us."

I am capable of apologizing. I did not wake up high. I make people want to write in a good way. I had a beautiful place last night. I don't have nightmares about my IUD perforating my uterine walls. My symptoms will remain under control. I did not embarrass myself post-karaoke. My friends show up for me. I am not as bad at poetry as I think. These affirmations are not a series of autofiction. I say nice things about you when you're not in the room. When I don't say nice things about you I punish myself and repent. I am not obsessed with penance. I am right to judge people who don't like Dorchester. I did not receive a pointed and entitled text from you. I once made a ceramic sun and it lives on the wall of my parents' house. That is not one of my happiest memories from childhood. Irregular bleeding is to be expected to the point where it should actually just be called regular. I did not forget about you but I did disregard your feelings which is probably worse! I will get paid. When I get paid I will buy you a coffee and you will love me again. I am sorry and I am sorrow. I am trying my best! My best could use some improvements if we're being honest. I am not writing this as a love note. I am writing this as sordid and self-masturbatory accountability. I am in love with you, though. The words just got lost behind the wrong confession.

I am learning not to self-flagellate in the name of amorous embarrassment. I am learning that some people just think I'm stupid conceptually and that's okay. I am learning that I miss you more than I gave you credit for even though I hate the way you text. I am learning that I am probably pansexual. I am learning that I remain politically forever lesbian. I am learning that that thing you did to me wasn't really cool even though I played it off. I am learning a lot about my own contempt for polyamory. I am learning that I have a "one who got away." I am learning that my confidence is easily decimated by men because I revert to patterns I learned as a teenager. I am learning about you through your iCloud email. I am learning how to carve a space for what I don't have. I am learning that emptiness is part of being full-grown. I am learning that I need to not get so fucked up that I say things that aren't true. I am learning to say things just for the sake of my own peace instead of with the expectation of reciprocation. I am learning about learning about love. I am learning about what I am looking for. I am learning so much through these godawful dreams. I am learning that some parts of my life may be over. I am learning what it means to receive true friendship. I am learning and relearning the patterns of your hand even though I can't touch it anymore. I am learning the way you love me is okay. I am learning I can get by on enough love. I am learning your talent! I am learning from what you say on your Close Friends stories which I am no longer privy to. I am learning how to forgive. I am learning how to clean up. I am learning how to go through life without an escape plan. I am learning the face of my own loneliness. I am learning the face of yours.

I exist offline. I did not profess my crush on the wrong person yesterday. I corrected my incorrect profession. I look good with a cheeseburger. When I touch boys I generally feel nothing. I am not avoiding lesbian intimacy because I'm worried about falling back in love. I am becoming a successful findom. I do not have $0 in my bank account. Or—I won't for much longer! My glasses prescription is not too low. 24 year olds aren't all bad. I was bad when I was 24! I am no longer that bad. My foot pictures will elicit a monetary response. I do not like you more than you like me. I am going to be with someone who knows they want to be with me on the first go! Someones are coming my way in a positive manner. I am not burnt out from sex. I am alighting a boundaried spark. My dog will see his best friend Eddie very soon. I can face the day! I am not malnourished in the realm of sleep. Wearing a cheerleading skirt does not make me a girl. I feel you out there. You did not dress up with me for a couple's Halloween costume in the same outfit you used with your ex. I wish I knew how to omit you! I would never write about you. I'm not writing about you now because you asked. I hope you're having fun with all the friends that are too young for you. I am a constellation of my memories. I am not stupid even when I make stupid choices. You will learn to love me.

My brain is fixed by cold water. There is no reason to cry into my milkshake. The guy who buys my [redacted] will accept my rates. He will also stop calling me a girl and learn some manners. People respect my boundaries. I am going to get new glasses and see better soon. I will not bitch you out over text. Proclamations of infatuation mean nothing to me. I am wet for people who show up. No one is lying to me right now. I am no longer lying to myself! It's okay when you cry after sex. I am safe like that.

Female manipulator music doesn't set me off. I am not late on the Doodle poll. I am vastly appreciated for my stunning personality. I am actually a little reserved in person. We were never compatible even when I tried to make myself into someone who could love you. I do not jerk off to my Venmo balance. I do not jerk off to my email. My sketchbook is full of genius ideas. I am not devastated that you stopped being my friend when I started being gay. Nonalcoholic beverages can't make me feel drunk. Tomorrow will not ruin my week. You are going to respond to the message I sent when I was trying not to bitch you out. I like when you breathe through your nose all loud. Babies can't hurt me. You weren't looking at yourself in the mirror while you fucked me. You were looking at me.

I am not checking for your name in my Instagram story views every time without fail. I did not spend the last week running myself into the ground sexually, emotionally, and physically. People are allowed to like vanilla ice cream without it being a character flaw. I am going to feel much better very soon. This is not the season of repressed memories. I will receive a day-altering invitation. I will recommit to taking my meds. There is nothing wrong with me beyond an average amount of wrongness. I am never going to pay that hospital bill. Nothing is wrong with me! Nothing at all! You did not laugh when I told you my red flags. People didn't forget how to hold hands. I am a generation away from the mines. No one will die before I can get to them. I am not looking for you through the hole in the blanket. When I let them into my body it's not you I feel inside. I am so much more than a booty call. I am worth every ring on my nightstand. I did not go through your jewelry box at your parents' house. I did not find an object that filled my lungs with something heavy. Every parent is just a person. I should never be a parent but I often think about what our babies would look like. I do not have a problematic height preference in sexual partners. I am not self-hating for being five foot three. There was not a part of me that was excited when that bad thing happened. Someone once told me that your greatest fear is sometimes your greatest wish and now that has become my greatest fear. You were never a good writer but I won't tell you that. Love is on its way to me.

I am going to get to you before you disappear. The retail value of my shoe store job slippers does not hurt when I think of their ruination in the damp vineyard of France. You will wait for me. The canine genetics of resource guarding can be undone with thoughtful training and the removal of triggers. I am not in love with you anymore but I am in love with who I wish you could be. I am in love with someone else and another someone and another someone but I am keeping that shit to myself these days. The smell of cigarettes eclipsing exhaust does not turn me on and remind me of a time before consciousness all at once.

Your lips were so smoky the first time we kissed, I almost regret making you quit. I did not ruin my new slippers by climbing into your car the other night and walking you back to my bedroom. Our shared dysphoria made me want to say I love you even though I couldn't possibly. Lifting my friends up is the most important thing to me. You could be my friend if you wanted. I am working every passing day on forgiveness. I miss my grandmothers when I open the door. I miss you when I stand in the doorway. I am not in the top 1% of listeners to Radiator Hospital on Spotify. I did not fake knowing that band in case it made you want to kiss me. I truthfully can't lie for shit and that is the best and worst thing about me. Lychee jelly explodes in my mouth just like you used to. I am capable of telling you when sex hurts. I am capable of telling you when love hurts. I am capable of discerning the difference between sex and love.

Attraction is not love! Scream it from the rooftops. I am not owed a French-Canadian girlfriend but I'd like one. I am going to treat my next girlfriend so well. I do not still wish that you were the lady of my heart. Was it ever about our hearts in the first place? I am not going to succumb to the cold of my body or the hot of my mind. I am going to improve. Self-improvement is not the entirety of my personality. Shelter animals get well with minor veterinary care. You are not the keeper of my hunger nor heart. You are just one more person in the stitch of my chapters.

We were never going to get married. I do not miss you my love.

I am not frenetically disturbed by my childhood romance. I have forgotten the first time I was called a bitch with no laughter present. Drinking juice is almost the same as being in a warm place. The Instagram stories in which Eileen Myles posts shelter dogs being euthanized do not rattle me. I do not regret an entire country. If I check my archived WhatsApp chats maybe you got back to me and I just missed it. I am not lost among the Yous. My youth is permanent. Dogs can learn up to hundreds of human words. Journaling is not objectively the worst coping mechanism. I do not resent the handwritten words on your poorly lined page. They forgot "fucking your roommate" in the seven deadly sins. You did not forget my dog's name repeatedly.

My dog has a memorable and dignified name. I like when the flavor is "confetti" because it reminds me of celebrating with you. You will not thumbs up react to my heartbreak text. I will make love in the house in the woods with someone newer and more beautiful than her. To me everyone is more beautiful than her but that isn't nice to say so I will keep it to myself! I do not tear up when I see the make and model of my parents' old cars drive by. I can identify individual automobiles. I did not fantasize about a life with you late last night. Our lives could never! And that is okay. I am not too transient for affection.

Putting roots down doesn't make you straight. My type is not cycling carpenters. Yes it is actually. A part of me will always wonder how you sound in bed. Mixing a bunch of different juices together will save me from scurvy. You didn't call me "Baby" by mistake. I would wager my dog knows upwards of 165 words at least. I do not want to give you children when I look at you.

Boys live in my phone and not under my bed. I am very emotionally intelligent for a sex object. I do not have a Virgin Mary kink. One day I will have a girlfriend who looks like an emo boy. Next time I see you you will be living. I don't need a hairdresser to be happy. I am not developing an avoidant attachment style as a defense mechanism. I have the willpower not to sext my therapist. Homosexual advances amongst dogs at the park are a healthy expression of excitement. The best concert I've ever seen in my life wasn't Grimes. Someone out there still calls me by my real name. I do not dissociate when I hear it! And I didn't tell it to you too early. I am not sweet and I hate being recognized for my accidental sweetness. I just have good table manners and prize human connection. I remember your old house. The painting you made me is in my childhood bedroom facing the wall. My grandmothers are on the other side of the window. I think of you with each little sandwich sword. When people nod it means they like me. I can identify almost any dog breed on sight because I used to read the dog encyclopedia in the school library. No one is disappointed in me at present. I do not want a mold of your dick for nights I get lonely. I tried being bisexual again and hated it. I am not a bad person for being a lesbian. You observe me with pleasantries not judgment.

I sometimes wish people still wore those corset dresses without being larping freaks because my tits would look great in them. I have never lied to you. I don't miss the tensed skin of your neck.

I can survive a rain check. The minor procedure was not the worst pain I've ever been in in my life. The nurse said "good" when I told her that but isn't that technically a bad thing? I don't owe anyone a history of nomenclature. My great aunt was definitely a dyke. Homosexuality runs in my family like addiction but I've never been able to abstain from girls.

I will not wreck a marriage. I look beautiful with dead flowers.

Men put politics before love but I put nothing before love so I could never be a man! Words are more than sounds. I am cherished on an international stage. I did not forget about your postcards. I used to read my mother's address book back to front and miss you. I have several binders full of useful pamphlets from the hospital. I continue to succeed at not sexting my therapist. I continue to succeed in general. I am an amalgamation of my failures which you choose not to see. You will not ask me what happens to me when the dog dies. My dog will live forever! My camera roll does not depress me. You can call me Mommy if it helps you get off. You can call me anything if it helps you get off. I have a strict and robust writing practice.

The locks on the windows aren't screaming. Someone once told me I'd never be more beautiful than I was at seventeen and that was incorrect and also creepy. I stopped drinking for personal reasons. Someone will invite me on a snowy picnic and we will play pretend like kids. I would not be a bad father. There is no rotting house at the back of my mind. I did not have a hand in the death of my childhood rabbits. I am capable of fucking people less than a foot taller than me. I like middle names that are also objects. I will fall in love again today. I will fall out of love with you completely. I did not check my archived WhatsApp threads in case you said sorry. You will probably never say sorry and that's okay. You told me your favorite flower was goldenrod and that is not stuck in my mind. I will find another golden boy.

I am the tape on your jacket. You loved the poetry I recommended. I lived an entire universe in the walk that we shared. Maybe I'm ridiculous! Maybe I am. But I have never said that combination of words to another person before and that doesn't happen very often. I want to watch you wear Crocs! I want to know your children. You didn't say the sex addiction thing was either hot or even a red flag and that made me feel like a person. Your eyes didn't make me feel gross and itchy. You asked me what I went to the hospital for. Your body felt like my body against my body. You didn't disrespect me a single time. That shouldn't stand out but it does. You liked my dog and he leaned against your legs which were clothed in pants patterned with birds. You said you were thinking about my eyes but I beat you to it. I am saving a kiss for you.

Jesus can't hurt me. I am utterly untouchable by semi-risen bones. My thong is not making my pussy hurt. You are, though!

The icons on my wall protect me nonetheless. I will not indulge in uncharacteristic passive aggression. I will tell you why you're fucked. Someone in this teahouse is falling in love as I write this. I am falling in love as I write this. I will not be indentured to projections! I do not know you quite yet. When I get new glasses all will be revealed. I have climbed the exorcist steps. I am not trying to make you jealous but you should be anyway. I like you because you also wear fur coats. I like you because you also hate my ex. I do not owe anyone friendship. I neither forget nor forgive. My Venus is in Scorpio for Christ's sake. The intellectual couple is not watching me drool over shawarma. I like to eat with my hands both food and flesh. Sometimes I miss having long hair but no I don't. A spoonful of anything helps me go down. We cannot know what is in the minds of others. I cannot know when you think I'm annoying in passing. I don't identify as annoying because I identify as mean as I have stated before. I would eat all manner of onions in front of you. I do not cry privately after glancing at your sneakers. I want you to always be cool. A woman once wrote fanfic of me fucking the Lady of the Lake and it made me feel weird but I laughed anyway. I would totally fuck the Lady of the Lake but not in front of her or anyone. It would be behind closed doors. I remember I have breasts when they jiggle as I wash my hair and I feel panic just for a moment. I want to lick the mortar between your bricks. Purple is the color of everything.

I fell in love! Which means I fell out of love as well. What a patchwork of love I am in. I got a bunch of gross texts from gross men and only got paid for some of them which bought me a Lyft that I needed after crying in public. My dog fell in love! He has fallen in love with two dog individuals. Their names are Eddie and Henry respectively. I didn't do that thing where I hurt myself when I think about you and instead I ate cheese puffs and cried in private. I hurt myself in other ways but I consider them to be much less severe. I kissed my home! I got a "glad you stayed" text. I co-wrote the tiniest book that will one day be part of a big book that will get me a lot of lauded attention. I realized I am not as stupid at poetry as I tell myself. I made my hookup listen to Blink182's greatest hits compilation on vinyl and I stood up for myself when I was treated with disregard (by you, as usual). I rediscovered my worth and love of dip as a foodstuff. I remembered the book *Sarah Plain and Tall* and I still fucking hate it as I type this. I am making a plan in my head for the autumn which I am starting to say out loud. I humanized babies through conversation. I ate a bunch of spicy food so my mouth would hurt so I could think about something that wasn't you. I love hurting! I made myself cum so well in a way that you could never. I did not delete our text conversation in between each new text. I warned a friend about the perils of love and the perils of you specifically. The constellation of Yous nearly drowned me this week but my addictive personality lives to fight another day. Someone who is usually creepy was kind. I suppose that's what they mean when they talk about the duality of man but truth is you're all pretty creepy in my book, boys. I saved my body for another time. I never do that! The granola bar felt too heavy in my pocket so I took it out. You don't remind me of my eating disorder and if you did I wouldn't tell you because that's not a chill thing to say. I listened to your favorite band and cried. Damn I am always crying. Life sure is a beach. No joke I am indebted to you for reading this and for asking me the question that prompted this at all. You are the face of love to me!

I am unfazed by candor. The people around me create beautiful things. You create beautiful things and I just have to tell you when I'm thinking of you like a kid with a funny crush. I create beautiful things. The things we have created are so different yet so beautiful it's almost as though they were made in tandem even though we can't pretend to know one another. I will not hyperventilate during my next blood test. I am not a bitch for having boundaries. The unnamed app does not have a disturbing misconception of what is hate speech. I shower with eucalyptus to cancel out the joints I smoke and it works! It is working. I can't pretend to know you but I wonder if your wife is hot. I am a valued member of Bachelor nation. My proclivity for reality TV does not speak judgments on my character. I would get a first impression rose. The lack of a dog park is not a hot button issue in the lives of my neighbors. I have survived through Google Translate. The bathmat is not damp before my shower. I might've gone a little crazy the other night in the DMs but hey! People make mistakes. Read that one again: people make mistakes. I went another day without bitching you out and that makes me a good person. I take the high road just like in that Irish lullaby. I am not too tired to think and I did not spend a day living in anger. I make the most of every day I am afforded. I am not deeply offended by responses to my question stickers.

My dog's tendency to mount new friends is not an example of trans-species genetics. I don't have to cum every time and in fact I don't want to. Maybe I'm saving some lost part of myself for you. This is not the same as journaling because journaling is stupid. Actually there is nothing wrong with journaling I take that back. I am not a bitch. I'll tell you one day the color of how you tasted. I miss you.

Writing these does not make me tired. I am pouring my heart out to a friendly audience. I am the beneficiary of passion. My hand will not go a night unheld. The kombucha in my gut cancels out the fact that I haven't been taking my meds. That's what the Instagram therapists tell me so it must be true. I did not skip a meeting to revamp my Hinge profile. My suspicions have been confirmed that less ass on Hinge equals less disrespect but what if my ass really is a part of me? I will fall in love this weekend, punctuated by both promise and boundaries. My bed is fresh for you. Daddy sent me a poem because I am a gift and I deserve the gift of words that I so eagerly dish out to you. I am just one person and my resentment can't move mountains. I am well-equipped to make changes to the titration process of my psychiatric drug cocktail. I am going on a secret vacation, a vacation inside. They will write Do Not Disturb on the doors of our heathen chamber and we will redefine marital bliss with our mouths. Boys are capable of emoting (I think.) My book launch is going to be a roaring success because I have been working so hard! I have been working so hard. Dogs under the age of three delight in my son. You have a real son, a human one I mean, but I don't know his name. I swipe left on everyone with the same name as my dog because that's normal. It is almost the anniversary of my institutionalization and I am all better! All better now. Saint Patrick's Day does not strike a nerve between my brain and my teeth. If we had a human son, what would we name him? I don't fixate on things that could never be. I have finished the Valentine's chocolates and am therefore self-partnered. Solo polyamorists can't hurt me. I have written books drunk on love; the books themselves are drunk. I only [redacted] my left wrist. I love mid-century tile. Someone is going to tell me they love me and scrape away the cobwebs of my arteries. I am not losing touch. I am inventing it.

I love crying! I love when you make me cry. I love the assumptions you make about me. I love the time you slapped me in the face. I love love! I can't wait to be whole. I fuck people in your underwear. I'm bad just like you thought! I'm so bad I'm good and I know you like that shit. Thinking of you! Postcards from my heart.

No creature has ever been wanted like I want you! You are the embodiment of my greatest wish: companion. Thank god Medicaid therapy was free in 2021 because I spent the whole time weeping about your absence. Now that I have you I am fulfilled. You are the infant I will never have. You are the delight of my day, every day. You are my sweetest muse. Even when I'm mad, we end up smiling. I honestly don't care when you hump your friends and I think they also like it! Your incessant squeaking of the squeaky ball never annoys me. No really it doesn't, I'm just happy you're happy. I'm happy whenever you're a happy boy. I wish we spoke a more common language so I could tell you how much I love you. I love your affinity for vegetables and how you climb into laps like a cat. Reaching my hand into your mouth to retrieve the trash you picked up doesn't gross me out because I'm just lucky to be touching you. Thanks for being here! My friend, my baby. Angelic boy who can't behave, you save me every day and I Am Grateful.

I always know where to start because I'm a Capricorn sun and I always know where to end because I'm a Capricorn moon. There is room to mourn all the dead. Lychee jelly will not give me a sugar rush. Genealogy doesn't frighten me. Neither does the age gap between my grandparents. I will not cry when the farm sells. One day I will give my dog a farm on which to run boundless. The germs on the doorknob are not after me alone. My psychiatric nurse practitioner likes me better than all her other clients and this is because I wrote her a haiku about having a meat share. I respect people with meat shares. Cabbage is no filler but a main event. Boys don't make me puke in my mouth.

The first time I ever puked in my mouth was as a teenager a few blocks from here! Silly how some things never change. My period will be normal this month after the Plan B debacle. The person who necessitated the Plan B debacle will break their drumstick. Is that too harsh? Probably not. You will not strip yourself of believability via text message. You will say sorry and mean it. I don't need to conduct time management for everyone around me. My stomach hurts for normal reasons. I am not inundated by DMs. I am capable of responding to your kind DM. I am going to get asked on a date. I feel it in the air! I will make time for love, sexual and otherwise, in a healthy quantity this weekend. Sex one day will be an act of love. You are charmed by me on Tinder which will translate to me charming you in real life. I don't know where you came from but I'm lucky! I will not eat every jellybean in a fit of rage. I will save some jellybeans for happiness. I am making my own way as I go.

There is nothing wrong with poetry but there is something wrong with poets. I will look sultry at the reading tomorrow night and you will fall in love with my voice. People disliking their birthdays is not something I should be offended about. I still fuck strangers in your underwear. I'm dirty like that! But I am extraordinarily clean because of my contamination obsession and that is also normal. Taking two to three showers a day is normal. You're in luck! I'm perfect.

My vibe is not unknowable. I have no use for lawyers. I will not send you the book I wrote about you unsolicited in the mail. All things are temporary when you are in a living body. I remember the first time I heard Sheryl Crow. I get enough vitamin C. I am not generationally deficient in other vitamins due to the potato famine. I'm sorry you're sad. I'm sorry I'm sad. I will fall in love tonight! I meant it when I said I like your hair shaggy. My dog's intestinal health is not compromised by his babyhood tapeworms. I can't be with you because you have the girl version of my dad's name. I know much about keeping leather shoes supple. I didn't keep your love notes. I will return to a city that hurt me but in a shroud of joy. I wrote my first novel when I was ten. People say you're so young to have a memoir but I started before I could talk. I am just the right age for everything except marriage. My god complex does not wreak havoc on all manner of relationships. Pre-packaged food is my friend. I did not start picking at my face when I realized you weren't interested in me sexually. I'm glad I didn't meet your mother; it would have made things worse. I am probably not the best to introduce to mothers at large. One day I will be! I don't have eczema. I just wash my hands once every three minutes until they bleed. I can only skip over my therapist on dating apps so many times. Your quietude contains the vague sentiment that you are rooting for me. I am rooting for you.

I know what "sfumato" means. I will not miss the love of my life this weekend like ships passing in the night. I am building a trove of goodness in the form of human hearts. I have no easily discernible character flaws. It is not a coincidence that Lana del Rey and "long distance relationship" have the same initials. The problem with my eyesight does not elude me. I look beautiful in tartan! My dog slumbers peacefully at the foot of my bed. He only barks at the voices of men. If I ever get rich, I will serve you a charcuterie board with imported salami. You'd probably like that because you're Italian. Every Irish person is not my cousin but it's true I don't fuck people with blue eyes. Okay sometimes I do but it's not my first choice. I believe in brown eyes being the most beautiful thing in the mirror that is earth. I do not have a complicated relationship with she/her lesbians. I always liked the color cornflower because it's made of the words corn and flower smashed together. I love an amalgamation. I purposely didn't listen to your EP until we stopped fucking because I knew it would be That Bad. I am no judge of music.

Flute girls do something different in bed. I never had period cramps until I got this damn IUD. Maybe I was lucky and pain was coming to me all along. The first time I got my period I thought it was a one-time event. Imagine my surprise when it happened again! I like to wear your underwear when I bleed because it's red and also fuck you. I am complex in my perversity. You will stay alive because I wish on the clock every day. I'm still trying to figure out what I care about. Someone walked by me on the street yesterday and I swear I could smell the deodorant you wore in high school. Someone is going to ask me on a hot Saturday night date. I am excellent at blow jobs.

Curtains are for hiding. You don't use my affection as fodder for your professionalism. One day you will see me in front of you.

I am capable of replying to your message of love. Oil on my back will fix me. The act of being is not a mental health condition. Changing my meds is going okay. I made a wonderful figure model because of the way my tits perch on my chest and my inherent flexibility of body and spirit. Dancing is not a prerequisite to having a wedding. I did not off myself last summer and that remains my proudest achievement as I prepare to achieve my dreams. Last night you were 266 miles away and I fell in love with you exactly seven days after I did for the first time. 266 miles has nothing on my desire. You won't read this and I'm glad. I never embarrass myself! Double texting is not a sin unless you're straight. I am getting meaner and more accepting all at the same time. A magpie functions as a sign.

What things, signs are. I will be paid what I am owed. I saw mustard yellow when you put your hands on me and I know what that means. My synesthesia is not a prediction. Despite what my childhood friend's mother said my synesthesia is also not for attention. Nothing I do is for attention except when I ask for it specifically. I am not a cold hard mommy bitch on dating apps. It's not my fault you suck at your own life. I have never drunk a forty. You did the night your friend told me the horrible things he did to a cat. On our first date my ex killed a rat with a hammer and that was normal. My ex's mom's aborted fetus has a cool name and I think of it every day. God is the original abortion! Thank fuck. I am saving myself for tomorrow unless you know unless. I shared a poem I wrote with you but I pretended it wasn't me who had written it. But you liked it! So then I said it was me. It was always me. I was born in the snow and the snow is my comfort. Next week is the five-year anniversary of my institutionalization and it will not set me back. I'm changing my meds because I'm doing so well. I do everything so well, including you. I would learn how to dance if you'd love me again. My hips know music but my mind doesn't. You said I was the first person to tell you about the loveliness of your hips and I regret it now because all of you is spoiled. I saw an apple in the snow and thought, "Love is a fossil."

My next love will be one of infatuatory balance. On Sunday god rested so I will too. I will rest in the lovemaking fashion. I experienced mortal fear for the first time in years! Usually death feels like a blanket over my head but this time it felt like a friend I don't want anymore. The only thing worse than nonmonogamy is monogamy. I only wear your shirt when I know I'm gonna get real sweaty. You never once gave me butterflies but one time I felt nauseous and mistakenly asked you to be my girlfriend. My book will not get me canceled. I will never date another farmer, but liking plants can't truly be considered a personality flaw. I am generous with my considerations of personality flaws. I am going into the mountains with people I love and you are not invited and it feels damn good. You should not ask people to be your girlfriend when what you really need is to throw up. I will not fuck your husband even if he wants me to. I am the bearer of all innocence. I do not drink too much hot chocolate. I do not drink at all and that is fine. My lack of alcoholism is not socially alienating. I was hoping we could just kiss sober. A present is arriving soon. If you ever get your hands on my book you will cry and yeah you should cry. No one gets mad at musicians for singing autofiction. Genre is a silly word. I no longer want to be challenged in love! Only worshiped. Life is a long thread that I wrap around my own finger; I cut off the circulation when I got to You. God I hate metaphor just say it like it is. If you are an allegory I am a fable. There is a precious lesson in entering my bed.

I woke up alive and so did you if you're reading this. I am endowed only with gratitude for your Staying Here. I want you like a double patty smash burger and sweet potato fries which is to say, hungry. I refreshed my email fifteen times in the last ten minutes to calm down. How can I be calm when I'm falling in earnest? Imagine if we'd never met! One night can change your life. The sharp objects are safely in their cupboards. I've seen your eyes before in a dream, no a person, no a cognitive distortion of lust and mutual understanding. I one day will knit you a sweater and it will be purple, never mind that I don't know how to knit because my hands are better at other things. Tell me how I please you. Come for the ass and stay for the true love. I am not crying! I am not crying because you're still here and I know better than to waste these days of knowing you. I drink iced matcha on windy days because I'm gay and have an appetite for fanciness. You have an appetite for fantasy. My body is not sore with memory but with remembering. My body is sore with passion. I can connect with people just by talking. I can connect with people without being high. I have many qualities that render me significant in the quest for partnership. I know what I am looking for (I don't but I'm learning fast.) You kissed me a necklace. There is no hole in my sock. I paid my psychiatry bill. One day I'll be Mommy to both of us and pay yours too. My brilliance necessitates darkness! I am allowed to say such melodramas! I am allowed to mentally fuck myself while you do my heart and body. Let's let it bleed.

I do not relish watching the neighborhood roadkill decompose. I do not miss the fetal beaver I gave to your sister all perfect in its jar. I do not have a proclivity for dead things. I didn't need you to throw a punch when my tits got groped by the Satanists but you tried anyway. I do not miss the tattoos on your hands. The first time we fucked I wasn't wearing America-adjacent underwear. I wasn't too high to remember the Kimya Dawson concert. I am happy about the cat's birthday. I am happy I didn't let you talk me out of a condom even though you told me it makes it harder for you to cum. I told you it makes it harder for me to breathe. I didn't break my no drinking streak because of the republicans at your graduation. I did not call you the wrong name during sex even if I did move my mouth to shape the wrong sounds at first. It was a nice save. You want me on your softball team. I didn't call your friend a two-faced bitch even though she is. I want to peel off your balaclava and kiss the face underneath. I don't wear my sunglasses purely so you can't see me crying. The girls in the psych ward were hot. I did not call you from a glass cell in the hospital and you did not answer. I can rewrite my whole life if I want to and call it marketable. I'm awful fucked for someone with nice parents. I am not a Brooklyn transplant. I'm from four blocks away and you made the rent go up. I want to climb you like the metal ladder in the deep end of the pool. I can give myself a breast exam and it doesn't activate gender dysphoria and an OCD meltdown all at once. Old people don't make me cry. I remember your mom's panic disorder diagnosis. You talked a lot of shit about your mom for someone who always had it pretty good. I don't care how your noise band sounds. I understand pop culture references. I know the size of the average pigeon. I do not make uncomfortably direct eye contact. I close my eyes during sex at the right time. I do everything at the right time.

Existence is not always an accident.

I have woken up every day of my life so far even when I didn't want to. You are keeping my things safe for me in your bedroom despite the fact that we don't talk anymore. I do not wish ill on your mom's mini ponies. I do not wish ill upon any living thing even your girlfriend. I am okay with dating people who are married. I am not wildly resentful of nesting partners. I won't ask you if you regret your child even if their existence was some sort of accident, happy more or less. I remember the first time I saw a cardinal. The photos of you on my camera roll don't make me want to die! I am attending events I committed to. You saw my call for help and thought seriously about extending a hand. My dog did not throw up on a blanket this morning. I'd wear a skirt again if it meant you'd make me your wife. When you asked if I was cultured I didn't stumble over my words. One day we'll have the kind of sex where you don't have to apologize to me after. The fake leftists can't touch me when I'm under the covers. No one can touch me when I'm under the covers because I am in the office of love and solitude, not even your ghost. I never thought your name was pedestrian like your dead friend said.

Yours was the only name I've never questioned. Some days I wake up forgetting that I don't know you anymore and this does not derail my progress. Pisces season won't kill me even on the anniversary of ubering to the psych ward. No one is lying to me and no one ever will. Everyone else's mental illness makes them compulsively truthful as well. I cut a butterfly out of my brain and you tattooed at least four. I did not fall in love this week and I never will again. Sometimes I think you're speaking to me through someone else's mouth. I have to stay alive because I have people to share in my successes. I always was Daddy when we played House. I never fell asleep in the planetarium. What the fuck are planetariums even for. I didn't need the stars until after you. Which one of you told me I look hottest in a white T-shirt? I wear black because of that.

I am not out of practice at love. I don't owe you four days of affirmations. I don't owe you anything but I went to Catholic kindergarten so self-disappointment runs deep. Fisting is a skill that stays with you for life. I once watched a pregnant domme fist a stranger's asshole while her husband said Good Job Baby and that's the kind of relationship I'm looking for. Sometimes I fall in love so hard I don't even need to fuck you I just want to sit next to each other and laugh. The best one-night stand of my life is not bicoastally dating someone I dislike from college. I can see when you're full of shit. Everyone is going to show up to our reading tomorrow night because I surround myself with the type of people who show up even on a "school night." I won't hold it against you if you don't come because I learned forgiveness in outpatient. I wasn't caught off guard that you called me gorgeous instead of a slut while you came. I know how to accept respectful intimacies. It did not lift my PMDD-induced deathwish when you held my hand. I don't need a PMDD diagnosis to know I want to off myself before bleeding. My psychiatrist did not communicate that I shouldn't kill myself via singing bowl. That would be a fucking ridiculous thing to do in a crisis. I left my crisis in Saturday. I'm healed now! The pack of babies holding onto one long string outside the window cannot hurt me. There is no symbolism in a baby parade. My sweetness transcends transaction. My stupid ex won't show up to my reading and if she does I'll read the chapter about how much she sucks for good measure. I can sensory process people talking on the phone inside the cafe. I do not begrudge you for forgetting me, only the abruptness of your text when you remembered. I am no longer enforcing longevity in relationships because I don't need you anymore. It is nothing short of a joy to share my bed in the morning time. I didn't puke! It is okay if I puke. Damn it those babies are back again but I am not uncomfortable. Everyone in my life is going to get better even if the cat ends up anemic. My dog is the closest thing I've met to an earth-bound angel. Do you remember when we danced to Sam Cooke and you whispered in my ear the line about marrying me and taking me home? I forgot how to dance after that. I'm not mad that you ended up sexy because I ended up sexier. Comparison is not a toxic trait of mine. Nothing about me is toxic. My blood runs gold.

I am loved for my chaos. I didn't zoom in on the dick pic to see what you wrote on your calendar the day you met me. The pets respect our interfaith household. Do you really think I like it when my own dog barks? I don't but I've heard worse than barking. You have a new girlfriend so I listened to your favorite album eight times in a row in case I can telepathically manipulate you into a love unbound. You don't know how to say thank you so you stick to sending me memes. One day I'll find someone who both does and doesn't mince words! My glasses won't get eaten this time around. You are allowed to project your fantasy onto me only once in an evening. I might be a slut but I always wear underwear. Your poetry does not give my neural pathways gender dysphoria. I had a hard time with children even when I was a child and that is loneliness. I've been waiting to kiss you all week. I don't know whether your allergy is made up and I'm too afraid to ask. I made up an allergy too. Lies aren't lies if they're the truth. I can handle people asking me for things. I was cured of my anger issues by someone with green eyes. The reason my zoom camera is off is not because I'm crying. I can submit to literary prizes because my work is appropriate for and palatable to all audiences. What the fuck is a mature audience. I learned a language for you and then forgot it about you. Sometimes it's nice to go home without you. Sometimes the milestones hit better without you in the background. For someone who's pretty good at sharing I didn't like when you made shit about you. Irish Americans will undergo a collective consciousness shift at midnight where we feel unity with everyone oppressed by colonialism and not for the sake of our own exceptionalism. My dog's name is not Italian. It literally isn't because then it would be "Vincenzo" and who the fuck names a dog that. Your lover doesn't look underage. If we fall in love I will make you bread every Saint Patrick's Day until I die even if you say Patty's instead of Paddy's. I miss you so much today and some days I wish we could be dead together. I guess that's how heaven was invented. One day someone will fling their arms around me and say Thank You until I internalize it. My sister told me she's the only person on earth who's not a little bit scared of me and she might be right. I hope you learn how to swim. In middle school swim practice we used to dive for heavy blocks in the deep end and when I clutched them to my chest on the way up I thought of you! I will follow you into the water. I will because I have no choice.

I am the queen of hickeys. This is a valuable skill. It is not surprising nor upsetting that we did not fall in love. I may be physically in the exact place I was a year ago but mentally I am Healed. I still think you're a bitch for rejecting my gift but I don't have to dwell on it anymore. I know how to tell time, especially on the clocks tattooed on my arm. I didn't reply to you because of normal reasons so you probably didn't reply to me because of normal reasons too. I am ushering in an era of reciprocity. I am allowed to bask in my own moments. My mind does not go blank when I'm writing these. Having new types of sex for the first time at twenty-eight is normal. I named my hamster after your favorite singer and subsequently killed it. I don't kill anything on purpose except for your sperm. I am not making judgments on the burrito options of New Hampshire because someone told me that was kind of mean. I am never mean on purpose. I am only mean in innocence. I found out you were moving through Facebook stalking. I wish I hadn't told my friend who stopped being my friend about how you stopped being my friend. One day I'll get paid on time. I secretly always want my toes sucked. I am not scared of our mutual addictions.

Neurotypicals can't hurt me anymore. My sexuality is not a temperate mess. The only thing that reliably gets me wet is money. I am not devastated by everything beautiful. I remember the name of your dead kid and I say it sometimes. I used to draw you hummingbirds because I thought I could talk to them. I used to play fairies with you because your best friend died of cancer. I wasn't making any of it up to make you feel better. I am comfortable living within delusion. I still have the hots for my hairdresser with the delicious buccal fat. My dog never bit his mother. I can commit to things! In fact, Commitment is my middle name. I will not force you into the shape of the hole in my life. I've always been happy in the snow and today is no different. It's almost like I don't feel the cold. The clocks on my arm say it's time to rest.

I am a selectively good person. *The Last of Us* is not an accurate current depiction of Boston, Massachusetts. I am allowed aspects of entertainment to quell my dissociation. It is a positive sign that my nighttime anxiety attacks are returning because for a long time I couldn't feel anything at all. I realized I love you this morning when I was brushing my teeth. Revelations happen in the pasty moments. My boundaries do not sound like ultimatums. I do not miss my eating disorder. I do wish I was capable of being your girlfriend but unfortunately for everyone I am no girl. I'm glad I never took you to Michigan because you don't deserve the northern Midwest even if your favorite band is from there even if you've never been on a road trip. Michigan is staying locked in my top drawer with the ring I bought you. I am allowed to gatekeep Michigan. I am not scared to be alone, now or forever. I planned my wedding today and it's going to be a scream! I've visited the New Hampshire parking lot where we broke up twice this week and I feel okay about it. You and your ex and your ex's ex and her ex before that are safely in Brooklyn. Your car wasn't hot. I didn't correct you when you made that fucked up joke but just know that I did in my head. I learned how to ice skate and subsequently forgot how to balance. I didn't tell you my dream because I'm afraid of verbally manifesting my intrusive thoughts by accident. My dad always says he loves me more than words can say and I don't regret repeating that to you in the dark. I am not damaged by compulsory heterosexuality. Swimming in cold water is always healthy and never an act of self-harm. I listen to the album your older sister used to leave in the car not because we fucked to it but because I still think she's hot. Your mom didn't notice my leg hair. I do not get off on apologies! That would be weird. I didn't ask you if you thought I was weird because I am insecure, I asked you because I want to see if you know that you attract fucked up people. One day I'll have a virgin guava daiquiri. My compulsions coming back could be reframed as progress. What an exhausting thing, choosing to live! I have no reason not to be loving.

I love you even when you don't watch the news. The water in my body is probably more like Thai iced tea at this point because I can't drink anything without sugar and that's okay. I was missed last week at the dog park. I'm not even projecting that, the straight girl who used to be on the swim team who walks the little sluggish dog told me. I'm glad you followed me from Tinder even though we didn't match. When the warm wind blows I smell your deodorant and think of your armpits and the paint on your pants. I taught myself how to have sex. When I told you about my Catholic guilt while we were naked in your attic bedroom you didn't laugh. When we broke up because I decided I didn't owe you my sexuality anymore you didn't fall asleep while I cried. My dog is a great swimmer and a persistent humper and that's genetics, baby. I could excel at monogamy if I tried. You think I look better when shirts cover my hips. I think I look better when everyone leaves me the fuck alone. Some days I stand too close to the curb because it reminds me of precarious nights on the train platform when I lived for the whoosh of something that could kill me passing by. I know where the local fuck ups hang out because I am one of them.

-

The dog at the dog park who has the same name as my dead dog is probably not evidence of reincarnation. When you don't text me back for a week I pick all of the hair out from around my nipples and that's normal. You asked me if I thought Kim Kardashian was hot right before I asked to hold your hand and that didn't throw my game off. I like when you gain weight because there's more of you to kiss! I am brave even at Zoom funerals. I recommitted to the lesbian covenant and now my problems are solved. Straight people will stop posting engagement photo shoots and care about trans everything soon. I'm not bitter and I'm not angry. I'm just observant.

My mom's iPod nano lives in our kitchen drawer because my dad engraved, "you are music to me," on the back. I'll take an order of that please.

Dreams are not punishments. I will be with you when you die. Nectarines can no longer break my teeth because I am no longer a child. I don't mind that you are an alcoholic. I am above subtweeting. Subtweeting doesn't really matter when you're lying amongst petals in the grass. I can live without having sex every day. I can live in general. One day museums won't exist. My EBT card will fix everything. My landlord is not a snake. I own one of those portable phone chargers. I would never trauma dump. Isn't it wild that both our families planted Japanese maples out front for the people who came before? I know they will never die. Normalize public weeping and weaponize public joy. Everyone will come to my poetry reading. Everyone will cum. I'm sorry I haven't written, it's just that I haven't had a minute to think and I really need to get one of those phone chargers. I earn my foot rubs. I would lie about important things but nothing is important enough to lie about. I am becoming desensitized to peanut butter. I will somehow inherit a farm with a wide yard for my dog to run. I deserve the flowers you bring me. No one ever looked back on their deathbed and said, "I wish I'd worked more." I saw the name of my childhood rabbit on a grave which means nothing. I miss your rabbit even though you were weird about her virginity. Rabbits don't have the construct of virginity. That is one thing that is good and right.

You gave me a silver coin once and of course I didn't lose it.

You are something I could never lose.

Acknowledgments

The author gratefully acknowledges the work of the following artists referenced in this manuscript: Maya Skylark, Eileen Myles, and Kimya Dawson.

To the DOPAMINE team: I owe abundant thanks to Michelle Tea and Beth Pickens for giving me the time of day, and all the rest of it. Thank you to Brooke Palmieri for the book design and Cate White for the cover art.

To the writers and mentors who offered their words on this book: CA Conrad, Nate Lippens, K. Iver, and Elaine Kahn: it is an honor to make things while you are making things in the world.

Thank you to the many people who have loved me through this book and otherwise. Particularly to my grandfather, Michael Rafferty, for allowing me to get to you before you disappeared.

An honorable mention to the endearing(?) disaster of Boston, Massachusetts; I would know nothing of love without you.

And to you: words fail!

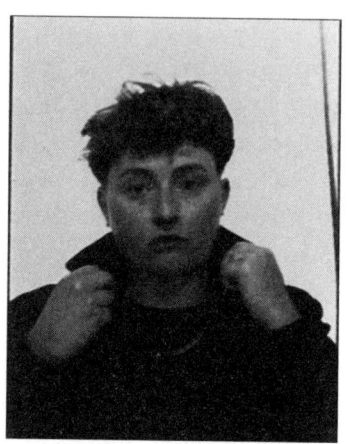

L Scully is a living writer.
https://www.lscully.com/